Ella's Greatest Adventures
"The Taste of Temperance"

Story By:

Ashley N. Thompson

Illustrated by:

Cristine Evaristo

Proverbs 16:32 "Better a patient person than a warrior, one with self-control than one who takes a city."

To all of my Adventurers
That loves to explore with little restraint
God has given you the ability to stop what
you're about to do, think about your
choices, and do what pleases Him

The sweet smell of cakes and cookies filled the house, stopping Ella from playing with her toys.

She needed to see what her mom was doing immediately.

"I'm baking these for our church bake sale. This will help raise money!" Ella's mom said cheerfully.

"This will also help fill my tummy!" Ella said with a smile.

The next morning, Ella and her mom got dressed to deliver the cakes to their church's bake sale.

Ella couldn't wait to help her mom sell some cake slices and to grab a few pieces for herself.

After Ella helped her Mom set up her table, the line for cakes was very long.

Everyone wanted her mom's cakes!

Heaven's Cake

It was a good thing Ella's mom baked as many cakes as she did, because everyone was buying plenty.

Ella was becoming anxious as she noticed the cakes on the table were starting to disappear.

Heaven's
Cake

It was finally the end of the bake sale, and thanks to Ella, they were able to sell all of the cakes.

"All except for one." Ella's mom surprised Ella with her favorite cake, banana pudding cake.

Ella's eyes lit up with joy. She couldn't wait to grab a slice of cake.

She ate her first slice and it was like heaven. Ella was ready for her next slice!

Three slices later, Ella started feeling sick. She'd eaten too many slices of cake!

"Ughhh, I feel awful!" Ella said while holding her stomach in pain.

On the way back home, Ella started to pray over her stomach.

 "Lord, forgive me for overeating.

Thank you for healing my stomach and making me feel better. In Jesus' name. Amen."

She then put on her faith bracelet and fell asleep.

Ella woke up to what looked like a bakery.

She wore a purple chef coat and hat with a mixer in her hand.

Ella had no idea why she was there!

A cupcake lady holding a tray of a dozen cupcakes came from the kitchen to the front of the bakery where Ella was standing.

Her hair was whipped icing and the nametag read "Ms. Sprinkles."

Ms. Sprinkles

"I didn't think you would ever come! I need your help," said Ms. Sprinkles to Ella with a smile.

"General Lee Greedy will arrive in town anytime now and we have to have 500 cupcakes ready for him."

Ella followed Ms. Sprinkles into the kitchen to help bake the cupcakes. It was a lot of work!

They barely made it to 400 cupcakes when Ella heard the chime from the bakery's front door.

"Someone is here." Ella whispered to Ms. Sprinkles.

It was General Lee Greedy! He walked in with a stern look and sat quietly at a table, looking around the bakery.

"I NEED MY CUPCAKES!" He yelled suddenly.

"We do not have 500 cupcakes yet, but we're–"

Before Ms. Sprinkles could finish her sentence, Gen. Greedy yelled at her furiously.

Ms. Sprinkles gave him what they finished and watched as Gen. Greedy ate the 400 cupcakes.

Ella watched everything from the kitchen. She was upset at how rude Gen. Greedy was to Ms. Sprinkles and how many cupcakes he ate.

 He had no plan to share and no self-control. It reminded Ella of how much she ate at her mother's bake sale.

Ella could not let Ms. Sprinkles suffer alone.

She needed self-control and boldness to face Gen. Greedy.

"I am smart, I am brave, I can do just anything! I believe and I receive, right now faith is what I need!"

She walked boldly towards Gen. Greedy who was now holding his stomach from cramps.

"Gen. Greedy, you've been rude to my friend and you're stuffing yourself with cupcakes! You have no self-control."

At first Gen. Greedy was upset, but then he realized how much he lacked control in his emotions and appetite. Gen. Greedy stopped eating the cupcakes and apologized for demanding all 500 cupcakes.

After Ella gave Ms. Sprinkles a hug and shook Gen. Greedy's hand, in a blink, she was back with her mom. Ella shared her entire adventure with her mom.

"I'm glad you've learned what happens when you lack self-control. What's next for Ella?" Ella's mom said.

"I'm not sure, but whatever's next, I have my faith for it!" Ella replied.

Letter From Author

Ashley N. Thompson

Hey Adventurer! I hope you've enjoyed Ella's Greatest Adventures! I love to bring joy and encouragement from my colorful imagination.

In **The Taste of Temperance** I know exactly how Ella felt with her love of cake. I loved cookies and banana pudding so much it felt hard for me to stop eating! I tried my own way but the Lord came into my life and started to show me where I was lacking self control. Talk about love!!

I'm here to remind you that you're fearfully and wonderfully made! God loves you and I do too!

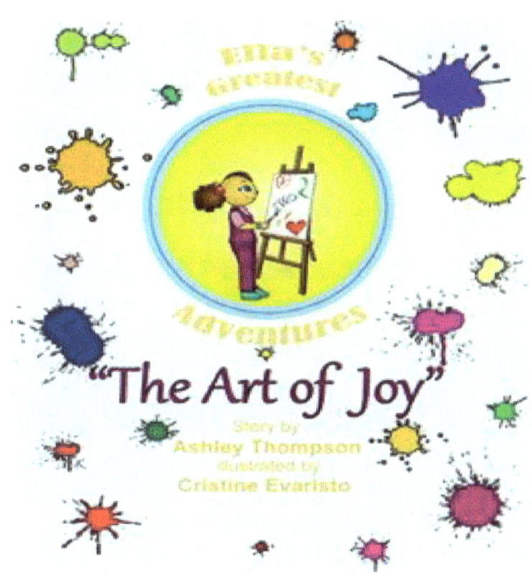

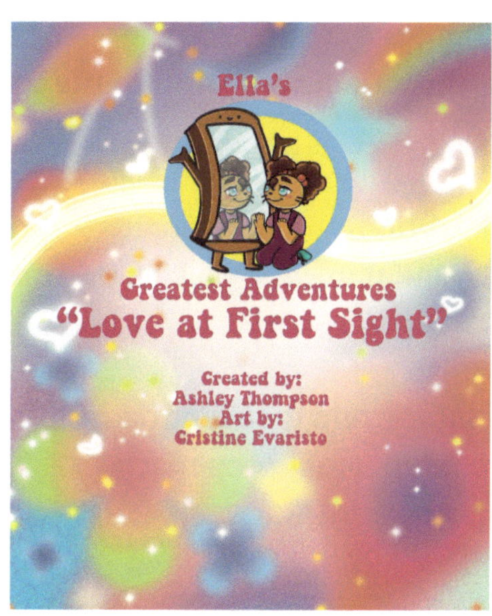

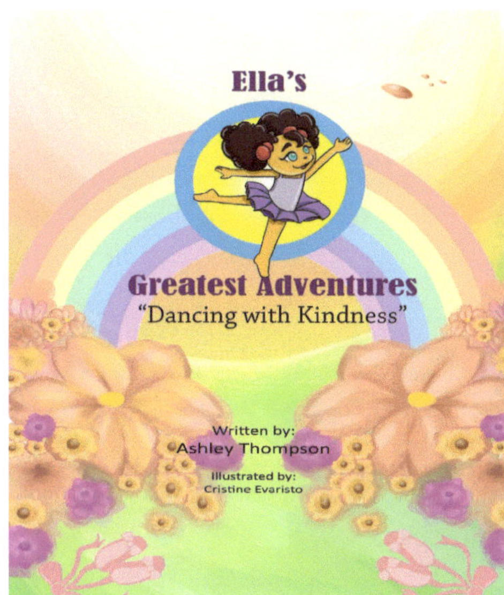

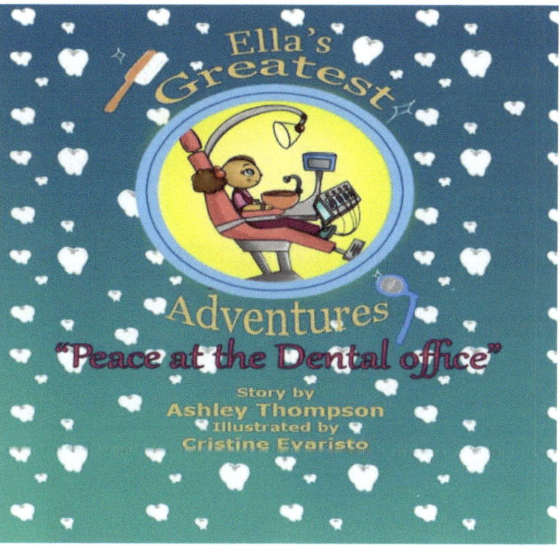

Are you ready for faith, fun, and discovery? Join Ella on every adventure along with your faith bracelet on

https://www.cultivatinginnerbeauty.com/ellasgreatestadventures

Illustrations by Cristine Evaristo

Printed in U.S.A

www.ingramcontent.com/pod-product-compliance
Lightning Source LLC
Chambersburg PA
CBHW042154030726
47599CB00004B/728